DATE DUE

MAY 15 2013		
MAY 15 2013		
DEC 17 2015		
	Discard	

Discard

Spies and Spying

FAMOUS SPIES

Honor Head

A⁺

Smart Apple Media

Smart Apple Media
P.O. Box 3263, Mankato, MN 56002

Printed in the United States of America

Library of Congress Cataloging-in-Publication Data

Head, Honor.
  Famous spies / Honor Head.
     p. cm. -- (Spies and spying)
  Includes index.
  ISBN 978-1-59920-358-4 (hardcover)
  1. Spies--Biography--Juvenile literature. 2. Spies--Juvenile literature. I. Title.
  UB270.5.H415 2010
  327.120092'2--dc22

                    2008049278

Created by Q2AMedia
Editor: Honor Head
Art Director: Rahul Dhiman
Designers: Ranjan Singh
Picture Researchers: Shreya Sharma
Line Artist: Sibi N. Devasia
Coloring Artist: Mahender Kumar

All words in bold can be found in the Glossary on pages 30–31.

Web site information is correct at time of going to press. However, the publishers cannot
 accept liability for any information or links found on third-party web sites.

Picture credits
t=top b=bottom c=center l=left r=right
Cover Images: Peter Hince/ Getty Images, Inset Image: Darrenwise/ iStockphoto: t, Q2AMedia: c, Q2AMedia: b.

Insides: Mlenny/ iStockphoto: Title Page, Pinopic/ iStockphoto: 4b, Darrenwise/ iStockphoto: :5t, Mlenny/ iStockphoto: 5b, Mary
Evans Picture Library/ Photolibrary: 7, Library of Congress: 8, North Wind Picture Archives/ Photolibrary: 9t, Keystone/ Corbis: 9b,
Len Green/ Shutterstock: 12b, Blue Lantern Studio/ Corbis: 14, Library of Congress:15b, Tim Ockenden/ PA Archive/ PA Photos: 16b,
Express/ Stringer/ Getty images: 17t, Iwka/ Dreamstime, Milosluz/ iStockphoto, ManuWe/ iStockphoto, Norman Chan/ Shutterstock:
17b, Library of Congress Prints and Photographs Division 20l, Associated Press: 21, Subsociety/ iStockphoto: 22tr, Nasa Langley
Research Center: 22b, Keystone/ Stringer/ Getty Images: 23, Keystone/ Stringer/ Getty Images: 24cr, Keystone/ Stringer/ Getty Images:
24b, Keystone/ Stringer/ Getty Images: 25cr, Keystone/ Stringer/ Getty Images: 25cl, Lanceb/ iStockphoto: 25b, , Alistair Fuller/
Associated Press: 27bl, Natasja Weitsz/ Contributor/ Getty Images: 27br, Associated Press: 28l, Len Green/ Shutterstock: 31.

Q2AMedia Art Bank: 6, 10, 11, 12, 13, 14, 18-19, 26, 29

9 8 7 6 5 4 3 2 1

CONTENTS

I Spy a Spy.................................4

Past Spies 6

Ace of Spies 10

Treacherous Beauty..................... 14

"The Name's ... Popov!" 16

The Spies That Never Were 20

The Cambridge Four.................. 24

Spies Today 26

Glossary 30

Index and Web Finder................ 32

I SPY A SPY

The life of a spy is one of mystery, secrets, and treachery. Many face the danger of discovery every day, and some even die. Others become rich and famous.

Why Spy?

People become spies for all sorts of reasons. Some do it for money; others because they believe in a special cause. People can be blackmailed into spying, or they become spies because they think it is exciting and glamorous. Whatever the reason, spies must keep their work and identities secret, often lying to their closest family and friends. They face danger every day.

Some spies work like burglars. They steal, copy, or photograph top-secret information.

What Is a Spy?

Spies or secret agents gather vital secrets, or intelligence, from the enemy. Then they pass it on to the people for whom they are spying or to the head of the spy ring, often called the controller. **Double agents** are spies who work for one country when they are really spying for the enemy.

Who Pays Spies?

Spies can be employed by a country, a political party, a terrorist group, or a manufacturer. The best spies are impossible to spot—you could sit next to one on a bus or in a restaurant.

SPY FILE

Qualities of a Spy

To be a spy you must be:
- cunning and ruthless
- able to think quickly under pressure
- prepared to kill people
- ready to face danger and even death
- able to speak another language fluently
- physically fit

Top Secret

Hiding in shadows, talking in code, making **dead drops,** and passing secret messages is the work of couriers. These are agents who are the link between spies and the people for whom they work. They have to be prepared to take great risks to pass on the most top-secret information.

PAST SPIES

For thousands of years, spies have been employed by rulers and army leaders. They are used to find out enemy plans and to give the enemy false information.

Ancient Spies

Leaders in Ancient Egypt and Ancient Rome used spies to watch rivals who might be plotting against them or even planning to kill them. Early Indian, Chinese, and Japanese emperors also used spy networks to gather intelligence and do away with enemies.

Cunning, silent, and deadly, fourteenth-century Japanese warriors called ninjas were employed as spies to carry out deadly assassinations and sabotage.

Top Secret

Some spies who worked for Alexander the Great (356–323 B.C.), wrote their secret messages on a piece of paper wound around a stick. The message was then unwound and sent to the king. The unwound message didn't make any sense until it was wound around a stick of the same size again—then the message became clear.

Mongol Spies

The mighty warrior Genghis Khan (1162–1227), leader of the Mongol people, conquered most of Asia. He used traveling merchants as spies to find out the strength of local armies and the weakest places to attack. The spies' reports were delivered by horsemen who rode with breathtaking speed across the country.

Genghis Khan's powerful Mongol army was able to take its enemies by surprise, thanks to information received from his huge network of spies.

Spy Networks

Spying played a vital role in the American Civil War (1861–1865). During this bloody conflict, families and friends turned against each other to fight for either the **Union** or the **Confederate** armies. Both sides used large numbers of spies, including women who proved to be very successful secret agents.

Southern Supporter

Belle Boyd (1843–1900) was a Confederate from a wealthy family. She started spying while managing her father's hotel in Virginia. Many Union soldiers stayed there and thought their secrets were safe, but Belle passed on all the information she heard to the Confederate army. She also learned secrets by going through the soldiers' pockets and **eavesdropping**.

Belle Boyd was captured by the Union for spying but was released in exchange for another prisoner.

From Slave to Spy

Harriet Tubman (1820–1913) was an escaped slave who could not read or write. She became a successful spy for the Union cause. In a dramatic and dangerous raid, Harriet used knowledge picked up by her spy network to attack slave plantations in the Southern states. She led several hundred soldiers in a raid, where they set fire to buildings, destroyed bridges, and freed hundreds of slaves owned by Confederate masters.

Harriet Tubman recruited former slaves and set up an information network that reported on Confederate army movements.

The new telegraph system grew rapidly across America during the Civil War. Spies used it to gather information by listening to messages that were being sent. This was known as wiretapping and was an important part of spying for many years.

Top Secret

ACE OF SPIES

Sydney Reilly was a great British spy. He was a master of disguise and brilliant at creating amazing stories about himself and his adventures.

The Real Sydney Reilly

Born in Russia, Sydney Reilly (1874–1925) was not his real name. In fact, no one really knows what his name was, as his official papers were probably changed to protect his identity when he became a spy. But we do know that Reilly enjoyed an expensive and glamorous lifestyle—exotic vacations, lavish parties, gambling, and the company of beautiful women. However, his taste for danger led him to a terrible death.

Reilly probably spied for at least four countries during his lifetime.

Secrets for Money

Reilly lived in many places around the world—France, the United States, Russia—and spoke several languages. He was a successful businessman and through his contacts was drawn into the world of selling secrets and information about one country to another. Reilly enjoyed the excitement, the sense of danger, and the huge amounts of money he could earn. He was a natural spy and was soon **recruited** by the British.

SPY FILE

Mansfield Cumming

Reilly was recruited into the British Secret Intelligence Service (then known as **SIS**, but sometimes called **MI6**) in 1918. His code name was ST1. He was recruited by Captain Mansfield Cumming, known as "C," who was the head of the SIS.

Top Secret

It is thought that Reilly changed his name when he married his first wife. Many say Reilly may have poisoned his wife's first husband, who was older and in bad health. Reilly's new wife was young and wealthy, and through her he was able to obtain a British passport.

Reilly was an amazing master of disguise. One report says that he dressed as a priest to get on board a yacht that belonged to some rich oil barons. He wanted to persuade them to sell oil to Britain. Another story tells how he disguised himself as a shipyard worker in order to steal weapons plans from a site in Germany.

Top Secret

Man on a Mission

Reilly's first mission for the SIS was to go Russia and find out as much as possible about the revolutionary **Bolshevik government**. But Reilly wasn't good at following orders. Instead of remaining **undercover**, he hatched a plan to either kidnap or kill Lenin, the Bolshevik leader. An informer discovered the plot and Reilly had to leave Russia quickly to avoid being caught and killed by the Bolsheviks.

Hunted by the Russians

Reilly continued his action-packed lifestyle, but he was now being hunted by the "**Trust**," a secret operation in Russia set up to punish enemies of the state. After a failed kidnapping attempt, the Trust tricked Reilly into returning to Russia in 1925. As soon as he crossed the border, he was arrested, imprisoned, and **interrogated**. On November 5, prison guards drove Reilly to a quiet spot in the country where he was shot.

The Russians sent a picture of Reilly's body to the SIS to prove that he was dead. They said that he was buried in a pit at Lubyanka prison in Russia.

TREACHEROUS BEAUTY

One of the most famous spies in history was an amateur and not very good at it! But her lifestyle meant that Mata Hari would always be remembered as a traitor.

Temple Dancer

Margaretha Zelle (1876–1918) made her living as an exotic dancer under the name of Mata Hari. At the beginning of World War I, the Germans were eager to recruit spies to help them win the war. They knew Mata Hari visited high-ranking military men all over Europe. The German Secret Service asked her to spy for them, and she agreed.

Dancing brought Mata Hari fame and many admirers.

Top Secret

Mata Hari's code name with the German Secret Service was "agent H-21." The French learned this code name. When they tracked down a telegram that mentioned H-21, they knew it was Mata Hari that the Germans were writing about.

Double Agent

Mata Hari suspected that the Germans didn't trust her, so she offered her services to the French as well. They gladly accepted and Mata Hari started to pass the French secrets that she learned from the Germans. But her career as a double agent was short. A telegram intercepted by the French revealed that she was really working as a spy for the Germans. The French arrested her and she was tried in a military court, found guilty, and executed. Although some people believe her betrayals were responsible for the deaths of many French soldiers, others claim that no one took her "secrets" seriously.

Mata Hari was killed by a firing squad. She is the figure in black in the center of the photograph below. Her body has never been found, and many people claim it was taken to a local medical school and dissected.

"THE NAME'S... POPOV!"

Everyone has heard of the danger-loving fictional spy James Bond, but not many people know he was based on a real-life jet-setting spy named Dusko Popov.

Glamorous and Wealthy

Born into a wealthy family in Serbia, in Eastern Europe, Dusko Popov (1912–1981) enjoyed a glamorous and rich lifestyle. He spoke several languages including fluent German. When World War II started, he was recruited by the **Abwehr**, the German military intelligence service, as a spy. The Germans sent him to England to work for the SIS to uncover military secrets.

Dusko Popov's official identity papers are shown below. But were they real or fake?

Double Agent

Popov hated the Germans for invading his country, so he became a double agent working for the British against Germany. He sent coded messages on postcards written in invisible ink to the Abwehr. The Germans believed that Popov was giving them important information. In reality, he only passed on what the British wanted the Germans to see. Meanwhile, any secrets that Popov learned from the Germans he passed straight on to MI6.

SPY FILE

Ian Fleming

Ian Fleming worked for UK naval intelligence, where he met Dusko Popov. When Fleming started writing his spy stories, the inspiration for the handsome, fast-thinking, smooth-talking British spy James Bond was Dusko Popov.

Top Secret

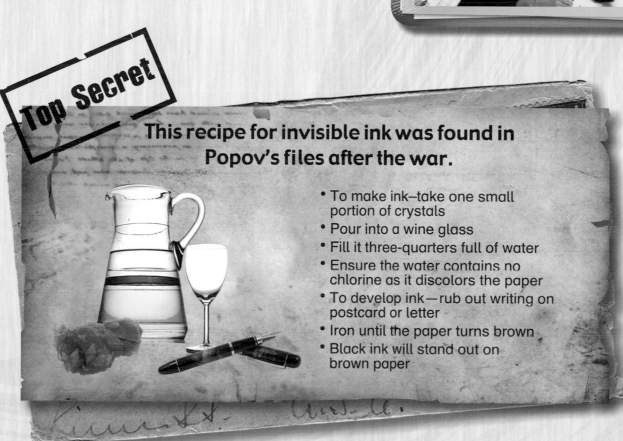

This recipe for invisible ink was found in Popov's files after the war.

- To make ink—take one small portion of crystals
- Pour into a wine glass
- Fill it three-quarters full of water
- Ensure the water contains no chlorine as it discolors the paper
- To develop ink—rub out writing on postcard or letter
- Iron until the paper turns brown
- Black ink will stand out on brown paper

Sent to America

In 1941, the Abwehr sent Popov to the United States to set up a German spy network. Popov contacted the **FBI** and explained who he was. He warned them that the Germans wanted to find out more about the American warships and troops based at **Pearl Harbor**. Popov tried to convince the FBI that the Germans might be working with the Japanese to attack the U.S. fleet at Pearl Harbor.

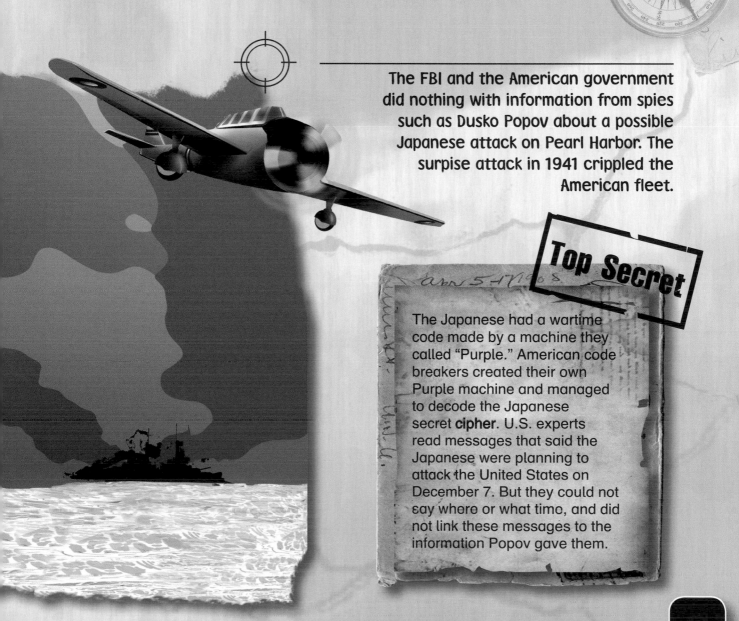

Warning Ignored

But the FBI knew about Popov's reputation as a playboy and his party lifestyle. They didn't trust him, so they decided to ignore his warnings, thinking it might be a trick or a trap. On December 7, 1941, Japanese war planes bombed Pearl Harbor. Over 2,400 Americans were killed and many ships and aircraft were destroyed or badly damaged.

The FBI and the American government did nothing with information from spies such as Dusko Popov about a possible Japanese attack on Pearl Harbor. The surpise attack in 1941 crippled the American fleet.

Top Secret

The Japanese had a wartime code made by a machine they called "Purple." American code breakers created their own Purple machine and managed to decode the Japanese secret **cipher**. U.S. experts read messages that said the Japanese were planning to attack the United States on December 7. But they could not say where or what time, and did not link these messages to the information Popov gave them.

THE SPIES THAT NEVER WERE

During 1953, two spies became the cause of protests around the world. The Rosenbergs were tried, found guilty, and sentenced to death—but did they deserve to die?

The First Arrest

In 1950, the FBI arrested Julius and Ethel Rosenberg on charges that would lead to one of the most famous spy trials in history. It started at Los Alamos in New Mexico, a top-secret site where an atomic bomb was being built. A scientist working there, Klaus Fuchs, was arrested for passing bomb designs to a Russian agent. Further investigations led to the arrest of David Greenglass, Ethel Rosenberg's brother.

Charges against the Rosenbergs included passing secrets about the U.S. atomic bomb to the Russians.

Top Secret

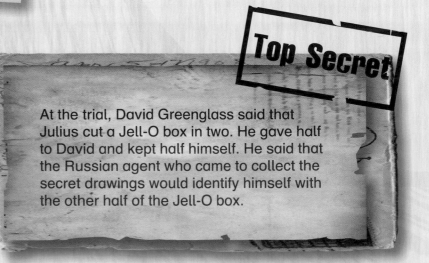

At the trial, David Greenglass said that Julius cut a Jell-O box in two. He gave half to David and kept half himself. He said that the Russian agent who came to collect the secret drawings would identify himself with the other half of the Jell-O box.

The Case Grows

David Greenglass claimed Julius Rosenberg asked him to copy top-secret drawings of parts of the atomic bomb to pass to the Russians. The FBI arrested Julius, who denied everything. To get Julius to confess, the FBI also arrested his wife, Ethel. The case against her was very weak, but the FBI hoped that to save his wife, Julius would talk. They were wrong.

The Rosenbergs were brought to trial even though many people thought there was not enough evidence against them.

SPY FILE

SPY TRICKS

The Rosenbergs were thought to be part of a huge spy network working in the United States during the 1950s. The network was run by a controller named Colonel Rudolf Ivanovich Abel, who worked from a New York apartment. Two of his spy tricks were to hide **microdots** in cufflinks and **microfilm** in hollow nails.

Nails

Cufflinks

21

Trial and Sentence

Julius refused to talk, so the FBI took both him and his wife to trial. The FBI produced witness after witness to give evidence that Julius passed secrets to the Russians. Julius denied it all, including the Jell-O box incident. There was very little evidence against Ethel except claims by David Greenglass that she had typed up the notes that Julius passed on. However, the U.S. press and public seemed to be against the Rosenbergs, and they were both sentenced to death in the electric chair.

Ethel Rosenberg was executed in an electric chair. The first jolt of electricity failed to kill her, so she had to be given two more jolts.

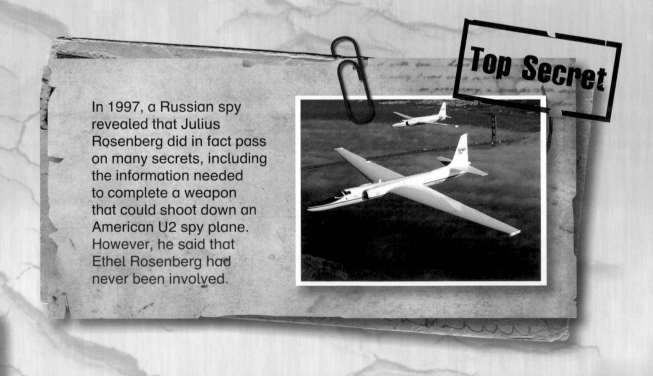

In 1997, a Russian spy revealed that Julius Rosenberg did in fact pass on many secrets, including the information needed to complete a weapon that could shoot down an American U2 spy plane. However, he said that Ethel Rosenberg had never been involved.

Top Secret

Protesters supporting the Rosenbergs marched in Paris, London, and eventually in New York.

"Don't Kill My Mommy"

People around the world were shocked that the Rosenbergs were given the death sentence when the evidence against them was so thin. Their lawyer fought for two years to save them. Their sons went on marches with banners saying, "Don't kill my mommy." Letters were sent to the White House and the Pope asking for mercy. But on June 19, 1953, the Rosenbergs were executed in Sing Sing prison, New York.

THE CAMBRIDGE FOUR

During the 1950s and 60s, a group of spies made world headlines. They were all well-educated, upper-class, and wealthy. One even worked for the British Queen.

Young Spies

Blunt, Burgess, Philby, and Maclean were recruited to become Russian spies while studying at Cambridge University. After graduating, they took up jobs at the British Foreign Office and the intelligence services where they could be of most help to the **KGB**. Among the information they passed on were details about the development of the atomic bomb and which secret codes had been broken.

Donald Maclean (1913–1983) worked at the British Embassy in Washington, D.C. From there he was able to pass on secrets about the United States and the United Kingdom to the Russians.

Anthony Blunt (1907–1983) recruited agents in the United Kingdom and delivered information from Philby and Burgess to Russian agents in the United Kingdom.

End of the Four

An FBI agent discovered that a member of the British Embassy was sending messages to the KGB. Burgess and Maclean were tipped off and fled to Russia in May 1951. Philby continued as a double agent for the next 12 years, then he went to Russia. Blunt worked as Keeper of the Queen's paintings until he was publicly accused of being a spy in 1979.

Kim Philby (1912–1988) was an expert code breaker. Philby was able to identify British agents inside Russia and pass their names to the KGB.

Guy Burgess (1911–1963) worked in the Foreign Office. At night he smuggled out top-secret documents that were photographed by a Russian agent. Burgess returned them next morning.

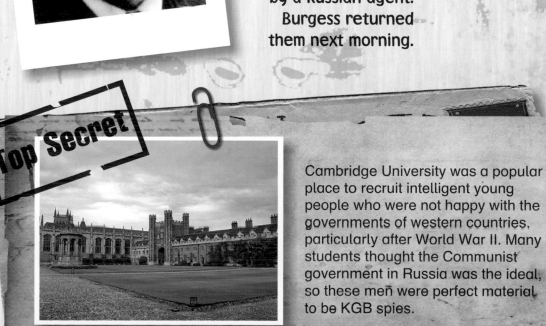

Top Secret

Cambridge University was a popular place to recruit intelligent young people who were not happy with the governments of western countries, particularly after World War II. Many students thought the Communist government in Russia was the ideal, so these men were perfect material to be KGB spies.

SPIES TODAY

Spies are used today by many governments to help fight terrorism and to uncover military secrets—and many make newspaper headlines.

British or Russian Agent?

Oleg Gordievsky was considered one of Russia's top spies. He was a master agent who had been working undercover in London for many years as a Russian diplomat. In 1985, the KGB found out that one of their spies was a double agent—could it be Oleg? He was recalled to Russia, interrogated, and given a truth drug—but he revealed nothing, and the KGB let him go. In fact, Gordievsky was a British spy, and he knew his life was now in danger.

When Gordievsky was ready to escape, he stood under a street lamp in Moscow holding a shopping bag. A British agent passed eating a Mars Bar. This signaled that the escape plan was underway.

Escape from Russia

At MI6, a plan to help Gordievsky escape from Russia was put into action. He was being watched all the time by the KGB, but he managed to buy a train ticket to Finland. There he was met by British agents who bundled him into the trunk of a car and drove him to safety. Once in Britain, Gordievsky revealed the names of many Russian spies in the United Kingdom who were immediately sent back to Russia. This was a big blow to the KGB spy network.

SPY FILE

Alexander Litvinenko

Alexander Litvinenko (1962-2006) was a former Russian spy who worked for Russia's Federal Security Service (**FSB**). In 2000, he fled Russia because he believed the FSB was corrupt. He moved to London. On November 1, 2006, he met someone for lunch and fell extremely ill. Three weeks later, he died from radiation poisoning. Before he died, he claimed he was poisoned by people from the FSB who were "ruthless and barbaric."

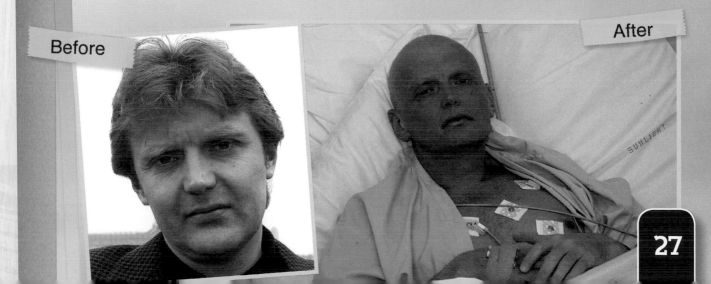

Before

After

Spying for the Russians

John Walker (born 1937) is an American who was working with the KGB to sell U.S. secrets to the Russians. For 18 years, Walker passed on U.S. military secrets to the KGB without getting caught—that is, until 1985.

Secret Plan

In May 1985, John Walker left a paper grocery bag full of information in a pre-planned place. The same night, the KGB left a bag full of money at a nearby spot. This is called a dead drop. FBI agents had learned that Walker was going to make a dead drop. They followed his van to some woods and searched through several bags dumped there, until they found one full of classified documents. They tracked Walker to a local motel, where he was caught with an envelope containing maps and instructions on where to make a drop of U.S. Navy secrets. Walker was arrested on the spot.

John Walker, a former U.S. navy radio operator, started spying as a way to make money.

The Trial

Walker was put on trial, along with his brother Arthur and his son Michael, whom he had also recruited to become spies. John and Arthur were sentenced to life imprisonment; Michael, to 25 years. John's ex-wife Barbara had helped him spy while they were still married. She was not put on trial because she gave the FBI information that led to Walker's arrest.

John Walker left military secrets and plans in a brown paper bag made to look like garbage for the KGB to pick up.

GLOSSARY

Abwehr the German military intelligence organization set up before World War II. Its main work was to gather secrets from foreign countries.

Bolshevik government the first Bolshevik, or communist, government formed in Russia in 1917. They believed that the workers and ordinary people should have more power and that wealth should be shared.

cipher a coded message in which numbers or letters are substituted in a certain order, so that the meaning remains secret from enemy agents

Confederate belonging to the Southern states in the Civil War. They wanted to be independent and to keep slavery.

dead drops a public place where spies can drop messages and parcels for each other

double agent someone who appears to work for one country but who is secretly working for another country

eavesdropping listening secretly to other people's conversations

FBI Federal Bureau of Investigation. It was set up in 1908 as a national security organization in the United States.

FSB Russia's intelligence agency. The abbreviation stands for Federal Security Service. It was previously known as the KGB, which was set up in 1954.